MOVE AND SHAKE IT!

CONTENTS

WOMAD:
World **o**f **M**usic **a**nd **D**ance   2

Interesting Instruments   10

Reggae Kid   16

Dance Crazes   24

World Of

Written by Janne Galbraith

Music And Dance

WOMAD is a festival of music and dance.
It goes on for three days.
Musicians and dancers
from all over the world
come to WOMAD.
They come to share music and to dance.

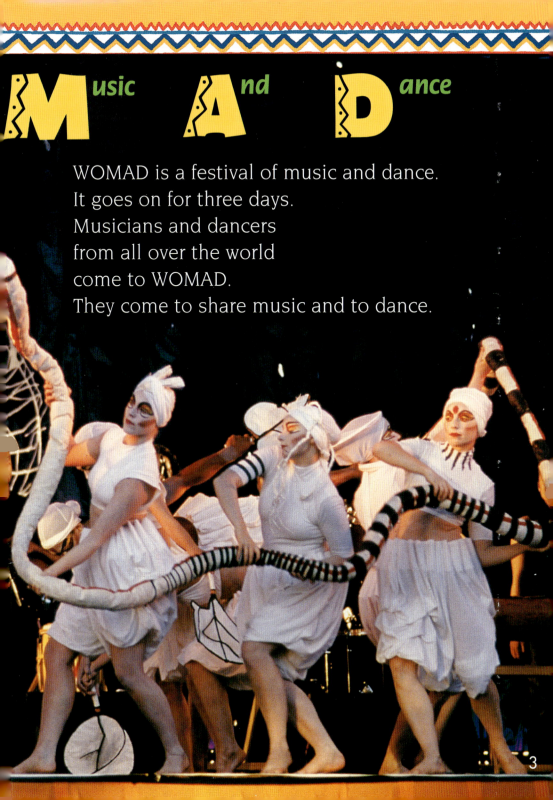

WOMAD was started by three men
who loved all kinds of music.
They wanted to get people
from around the world
together to share music.
They thought that sharing music
would help people learn about one another.
They thought that sharing music
would help people understand their differences.

The first WOMAD festival was in 1982.
It goes around the world,
taking wonderful sounds with it.
New sounds are added
as it goes.

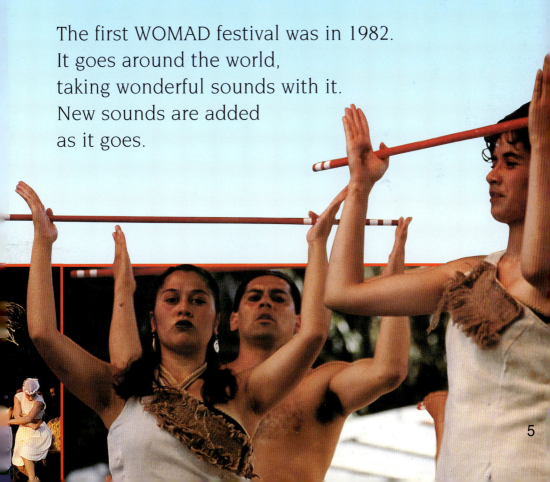

At WOMAD, you will hear singers
you may not have heard before.
The singers are famous
in their own countries.

You will hear many instruments.
Some make sounds
you may not have heard before.
The instruments are popular
in other countries.

You will see dancers
you may not have seen before.
Some of the dancers are famous
in their own countries.

Why might some performers be famous only in their own country?

7

All kinds of musicians can meet at WOMAD and talk about the music they make.

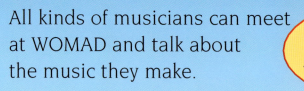

Which instrument would you like to learn from a famous musician?

The musicians at WOMAD teach classes. You can learn about instruments and different kinds of music. You can try the instruments and make your own music. The classes are lots of fun.

There are lots of stages at WOMAD.
You can walk from one stage to another
and see something different at each one!

There are so many performers
that the music and dancing
go on all day and into the night.
When it gets dark, there is a big show.
Some famous people
perform for the crowd.
The show on the last night
is like a big party.
Everyone dances and has a good time.

Interesting INSTRUMENTS

Written by Pippa Carling

Huff, Puff, Blow

Instruments that you blow are called wind instruments. All around the world, they come in interesting shapes and sizes.

Sheng

(China)
This instrument is a kind of mouth organ. It has been played for thousands of years.

Nose Flute

(Pacific Islands)
Some pipes can be played with your nose. Put one end in your nose and blow!

🎵 Bagpipes 🎵

(Scotland)
Bagpipe players blow air into a bag that they hold under their arms. Then they squeeze the bag to make long sounds.

🎵 Didgeridoo (de je ree DOO) 🎵

(Australia)
This instrument is made from a long, hollow branch. It makes a long, deep sound.

Rub, Pluck, Strum

These instruments are called stringed instruments. They are played by rubbing, plucking, or strumming the strings with your fingers, a pick, or a bow.

Lute

(China)
All over the world, people sing and dance to the sound of the lute. Lutes are pear-shaped.

Hey, look at the triangular instrument. What other shapes could instruments be made into?

♪ Koto (KO to) ♫

(Japan)
This instrument is called a koto. It is nearly two metres long and has thirteen strings!

♪ Balalaika (bel la LIE ka) ♫

(Russia)
Stringed instruments come in different shapes. This one is the shape of a triangle. It has a flat back to give it a special sound.

Clang, Crash, Bang

Drums are percussion instruments. They can be hit with a stick, a brush, or your hand to give your song rhythm (RIH thim)!

Slit Drum

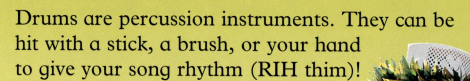

(Pacific Islands)
These drums are made out of wood. You play them with a stick.

Steel Drum

(West Indies)
These drums are made from oil drums. The top of the drum is shaped to make different sounds.

Xylophone (ZIE la fone)

(Africa)
Large wooden pegs laid across tree trunks give this xylophone a special sound.

Marching Drum

(Europe)
Long ago, armies went into battle to the beat of the drum. Today, drummers in marching bands play at special events such as parades.

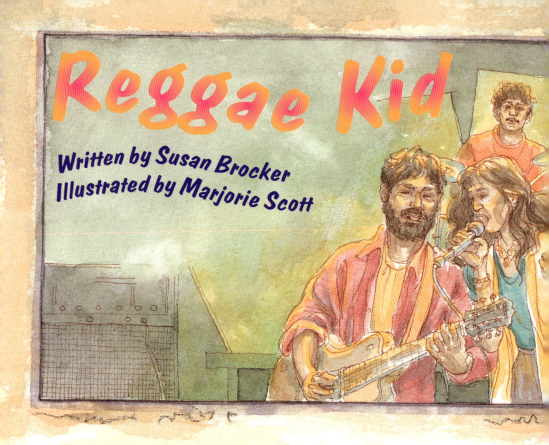

Reggae Kid

Written by Susan Brocker
Illustrated by Marjorie Scott

My Uncle Jack plays in a reggae (reh gay) band.
He plays the bass guitar.
I like the band.
I like the sound of reggae.
It has a happy beat.
But, most of all,
I like the sound of Uncle Jack's bass guitar.
He calls it Baba.
He can really play that guitar.

When I was very little,
I would sit down with Baba.
I would play it.
Uncle Jack would say,
"Kid, you are good.
When you are big, you can be in the band."

But that guitar was so big
and I was so little!
I didn't think I would ever be
brave enough to go onstage.

One day, Uncle Jack said to me,
"Kid, how would you like to go
to Jamaica (Juh MAY kuh)?
We need your help with our bags."

Jamaica is the home of reggae.
It's where Bob Marley came from.
He was the most famous
reggae musician of all time.
Uncle Jack was going to play at a festival.

Jamaica was beautiful.
There were lots of sandy beaches
and green hills.
There was music everywhere.
There was music coming from the markets.
There was music coming from the buses.
There was music coming from the people.

But parts of Jamaica were also very poor.
Reggae came from the poor parts.
When Bob Marley was a little boy,
he heard the poor people
singing folk songs.
He also heard new music from America.
He put the sounds together.
He wrote songs about hope and love.

The festival was three days long.
Musicians came from
all around the world to play.
People came from
all around the world to hear them.
People danced and sang all through the night.

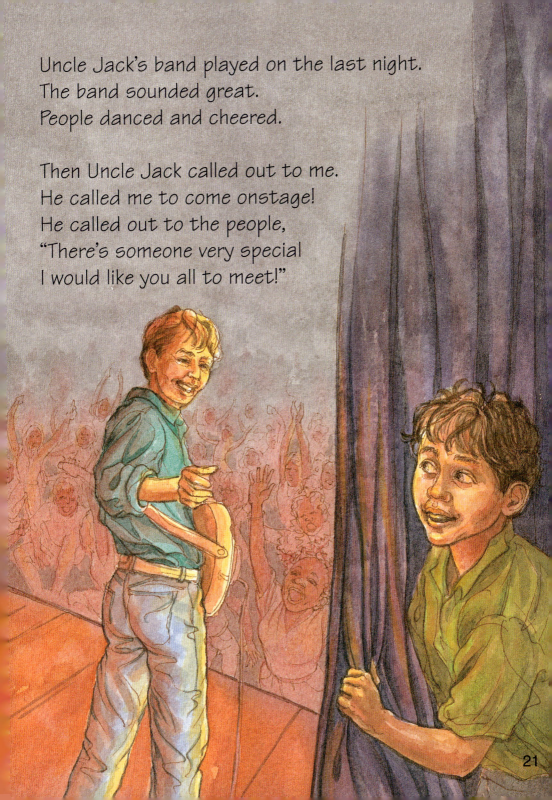

Uncle Jack's band played on the last night.
The band sounded great.
People danced and cheered.

Then Uncle Jack called out to me.
He called me to come onstage!
He called out to the people,
"There's someone very special
I would like you all to meet!"

Uncle Jack gave me Baba.
The guitar was so big.
I was scared in front of all the people.

But then I remembered the words
from the Bob Marley song.

I sang the words as I played Baba.
Don't worry about a thing,
'Cause every little thing gonna be all right.
Singing, don't worry about a thing,
'Cause every little thing gonna be all right!

The people cheered.
It was a great night.
It was a night I will always remember.

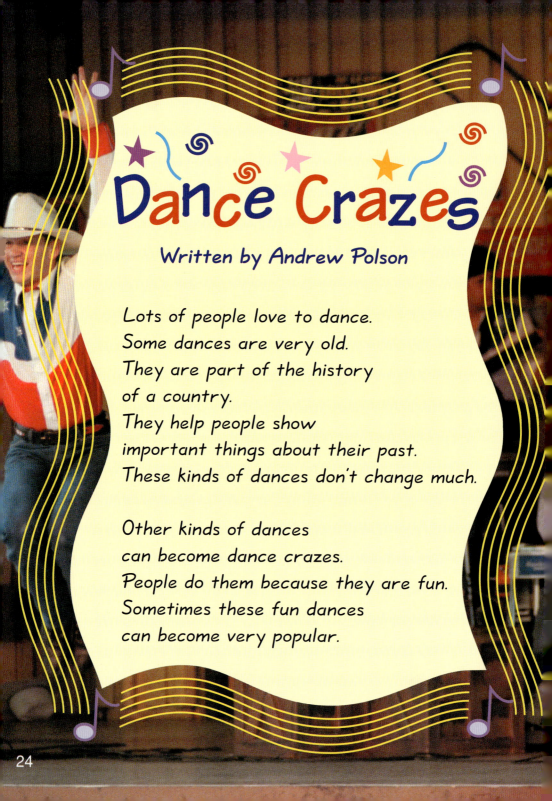

Dance Crazes

Written by Andrew Polson

Lots of people love to dance.
Some dances are very old.
They are part of the history
of a country.
They help people show
important things about their past.
These kinds of dances don't change much.

Other kinds of dances
can become dance crazes.
People do them because they are fun.
Sometimes these fun dances
can become very popular.

The tango is a very old dance
that came from South America.
By 1915, it had become very popular.
People went to special tango dances
called Tango Teas.
They were held at grand hotels.

In the 1920s,
a dance started in a town
in America called Charleston.
They named the dance
after the town.
This dance is fast
and has lots of high kicks.
People loved it.
This dance craze
swept around the world.

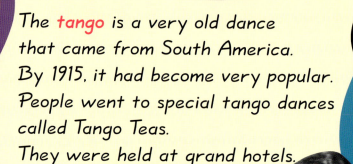

The Charleston could get really wild.
Some dance halls had signs saying PCQ
(Please Charleston Quietly).

In the 1930s and 1940s, a kind of music called swing was popular. People danced the **jitterbug** to this music.

The **twist** started a dance craze in the 1960s. A singer named Chubby Checker started the twist. Most dances before the twist had two people dancing together. But people could "twist" on their own.

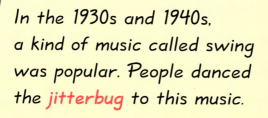

Do the twist! Move your hips and hands as if you are drying your back with a towel. Then move your foot as if you are grinding something into the ground.

The jitterbug is a fast, high-energy dance. Partners swing and jump.

In 1977, a movie called
Saturday Night Fever
made **disco** popular.
People would go to dance clubs
called *discotheques* (dis ko teks).
The clubs had bright lights
and people dressed in bright clothes.
People had disco dancing contests.

In the 1980s, people played music
and danced on the streets.
Some did **break dancing**.
Break-dancers did flips and spins.
They had to be careful
when doing this kind of dancing.

Today, there are lots
of different kinds of dances.
You can learn to do
any of these dances,
or you can make up your own!

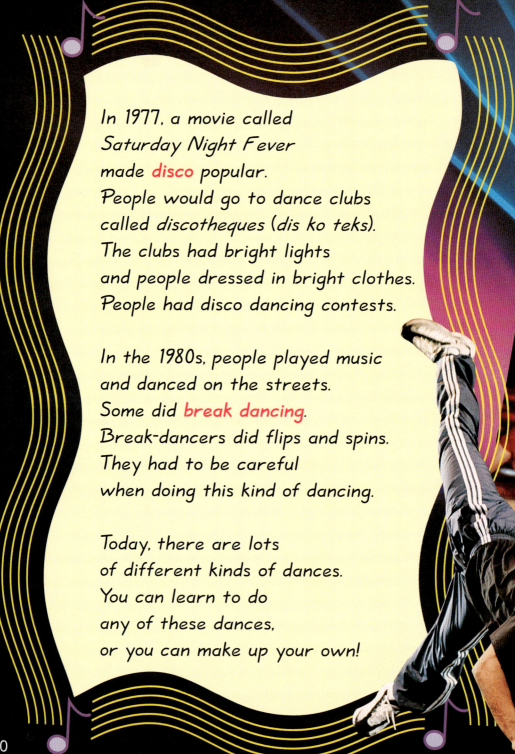

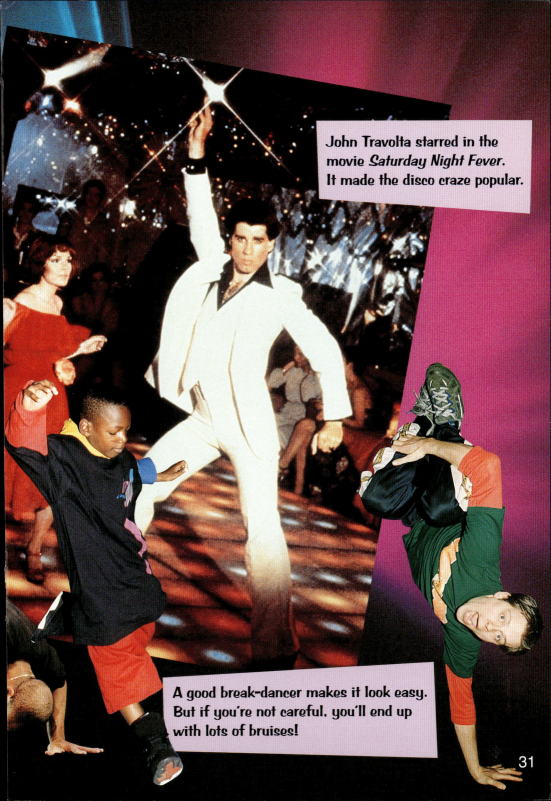

John Travolta starred in the movie *Saturday Night Fever*. It made the disco craze popular.

A good break-dancer makes it look easy. But if you're not careful, you'll end up with lots of bruises!

Index

classes	8
dance	3, 6, 9, 24–31
break dancing	30–31
Charleston	26
disco	30–31
jitterbug	28–29
tango	26–27
twist	28
discotheques	30
instruments	6, 8, 10–15
bagpipes	11
balalaika	13
didgeridoo	11
guitar	16–17, 22
koto	13
lute	12
marching drum	15
nose flute	10

percussion	14–15
sheng	10
slit drum	14
steel drum	14
stringed	12–13
wind	10–11
xylophone	15
musicians	3, 8
reggae	16, 18–19
Saturday Night Fever	30–31
singers	6
stages	9
Travolta, John	31
WOMAD	3–9